The Sculler

By

Leon James Fletcher

Dedicated to Adrian Stott my former coach and surrogate dad.

Copyright Leon James Fletcher

Cutting the Meniscus

The dawn has risen before the alarm at 5.30 am and a brightening June morning had started without many seeing its first light. A few early risers got to see this first light rising from the east with the sun rising over Putney Bridge's grey stone and the Thames murky brown waters that swirl between its buttresses ferociously when the current is high, bulging at the buttress before ripping through and downstream to the Houses of Parliament and Tower Bridge. Putney high street runs off the bridge and rises up the start of an impressive hill towards Wimbledon and its famous tennis courts.

Maybe a few players there had raised themselves from slumber or even been anticipating the alarm eager to go and practice their swing? Did they still love it or was the prize money the draw? This anticipated alarm held no financial gain but a love verging on addiction and a mesmerising exhilarating feeling of sitting on top of a boat gliding on top of a meniscus. Not sitting in a boat in the water but being on top of the boat almost hovering above the water gliding along the surface of the water only just getting wet.

Having sprang out of bed with a flourish of the duvet being whipped off as a magician would wave his cape, in an untidy room with kit and a few free weights strewn around, the sculler had pulled on his kit and headed off to the river. There was no time to tidy the room days were filled with training, eating and resting. All other time was spent visualising and savouring the feeling of hooking in at the catch with loose straight arms and then the back taking the strain loosely as the legs pressed down starting an unfurling of the body almost like a whip lash to the finish.

Half way through the stroke and the whip lash the back and lateral muscles started to squeeze with pressure and power developed over many miles and hours in a cold and draughty gym. Then with a climactic sensation the blades would be tapped down at the handles and leave the water, with a neat hole behind the spoon and be lifted square out of the hole while a tight core held the body suspended. The blades would be feathered on the return to the catch as the body recoiled and eased its way back in a rhythmic loop and the boat cut through the meniscus of the water and rose underneath the sculler as if writhing in a sensuous rhythm, as the sculls were about to be neatly dropped in at the catch again.

The night before the scullers girlfriend had laid on his chest and listened to his heart thudding out a beat of thirty two beats a minute and thought how special it was to be living with such a fit guy but then without explanation the heart rate had jumped to over one hundred and fifty beats a minute.

"What are you thinking about? She had said.

"You don't want to know." He had replied but after being pushed admitted to recalling the way Chris Ballieu a former World Champion had shortened his stroke at Chiswick Eyot and gone over the top of choppy water in the Wingfield sculls but the other scullers had got bogged down by the water by letting the boat be in it rather than on top of it.

As he cycled down Norroy Rd avoiding the High street with all its consumerism and materialism, he started singing "And I think to myself what a wonderful world" as the adrenaline pumped in the milky morning sunshine. The route took him down through the sought after road up from the Half Moon pub with a certain je ne se pas that gave it significantly higher prices than the adjoining roads. Still the song continued to be the back drop of morning joy as he headed for the club and the water.

At the club with a white panelled balcony off an oak clad hall, with black iron supports holding the balcony on the outside, the penultimate in a row of pretty boat houses and over looked by the large leafy trees of Bishops Park, he chained his bike in an autonomous routine as a slight anxiety gripped like stage fright as he prepared to put himself through what training program he had planned determinedly the night before. He looked at the Thames at Putney with the string of boats facing towards Putney Bridge.

There were no crowds on the embankment that morning or part timers just the purists and the murmuring of a rising tide. With a slow deep intake of breath and an overhead stretch of his arms he studied the Tideway in calculating anticipation of the morning scull. The Tide had not yet reached the concrete and was still on the shale but it meant that he could head above Richmond lock and on to Teddington as the tide would be over the lock by the time he reached it.

A few circles of the hips and he thought of the river tramp above Richmond who had moored at the Black Buoy in Putney for a few weeks and asked for water at Imperial College Boat House with a clean crisp accent and blazing blue eyes. The sculler regularly passed his floating home like a paddle steamer disturbing Huckleberry Flynn at around seven O'clock every morning. The sculler would even make an extra effort to scull perfectly past without any unnecessary sound of blades hitting the water or any dirty finishes so as not to disturb the man he rather admired.

Stretches over and brief anxieties, fleeting excuses and a feeling of dread in the pit pf the stomach subsided and the sculler picked up his oars, sculls or blades and took them bare foot and tip toe down to the water's edge. Then with a flex and slight strain back up the Embankment to take the boat off the rack before the tide can reach the sculls. The boat was housed at the back of IC's boat house and in the gap of Thames RC old ram shackled gym. The sculler loved training in this gym as he had trained in it as a Juniour and was comfortable with the lack of sleekness. There was toughness in its austerity and hardness in the winter cold, there was victory in its walls not comfort and privilege but sweat and blood.

The boat was kept on scaffold and at shoulder height which was perfect for one just had to place ones head underneath it and then lift and slide out from the rack. The boat was then balanced on the head like an African woman fetching water to her village. The boat was taken to the water with an ease through tight gaps that came with countless times of practice.

As the sculler reached the road between the club and the river his ears pricked listening for cars and any late comers speeding along the Embankment and then down the concrete to the shale where the scullers toes would curl feeling for any sharp stones and he tip toed down to the water's edge. The boat then was rolled off the head gracefully onto the water after stepping into the Thames water above the ankles with the faith of a Ganges worshipper or a Harijan (untouchable) the water was not feared but embraced even if not intentionally drank.

The bows of the boat were tipped into the shore so the incoming tide could not "grab" them and swing the boat out into the middle of the river while the sculler picked up his sculls from the shale. Using the blade handle to keep the boat positioned the sculler put his sculls into the gates of the riggers. Red scull for the right hand and green for the left then placing one foot onto the decking between the slides the sculler pushed off sending a wave out parallel to the bank and then using the tide let the stream take the boat out from the bank and towards the pretty string of boats by the black buoy while putting his feet into the training shoes fixed into the boat on the stretcher.

Strictly speaking one should scull down passed London Rowing club at the far end of the line of clubs and towards Putney pier to navigate to the centre of the incoming tide but skill, confidence and rebelliousness left the sculler comfortable to turn between the boats and miss the boring part of the outing. As the bow of the boat hit the point level with the string of boats a few sharp tugs on the left scull would easily spin the boat to be facing the right direction and then the exercise would begin.

Sitting at back stops the sculls were circled in at the catch and immediately tapped out at the finish a reminder of the basics of sculling hands, body slide, then the reverse legs (slide) body and finally hands squeezing out the finish which had been accelerated from the catch. The perfect catch was once metaphorically imagined to be like sitting on the toilet and tearing off one piece of toilet roll hanging on the door in front. Just a circle of the hands and the blade should drop in or circle into the point of furthest reach.

Sculling and sport in general is about getting the maximum out of the minimum effort, so that when maximum effort is applied the maximum speed or distance is achieved smoothly and gracefully disguising the inner agony of the competitor. Most people have seen the boat race between Oxford and Cambridge and seen how at the finish line near perfect oarsmen collapse in agony as the finish line is reached even in victory. It has also been said of crew rowing that the one sat behind the other thinks of themselves as better than the one in front or even heard to cry out:

"Row like me!" an Oxford blue rowing in the National squad eight. The sculler had none of that. No one to blame, no one else to take the credit or to fit in with but just the boat, the blades and the water linked together in a repetitive and an all-consuming rhythm. Needless to say "Row like me" was never seen in a single scull.

Having built the stroke up through the slide the sculler set off to Teddington a session that would take well over a couple of hours. The sculler had recently met his friend Mikhail Ivanov, who was Ukrainian and a World Champion for CCCP or Soviet Union in quad sculls, at a training camp in southern Italy. The Russians were training over four hours a day and the Sculler had decided to try and match this with the inspiration of Mike Spraklen, Sir Steve Redgrave's former coach.

At times the sculler would concentrate on technique or look at his puddles disappearing into the distance and the spacing between them but often his mind would be numbed as the rhythm embraced him and his mind could let his subconscious self, take care of the sculling. To the annoyance of some he had won the Physics prize at School and was thought not to study but at the time:

"V squared equals U squared plus two multiplied by A multiplied by S." and "F equals M multiplied by A." had been going through his mind even playing with Newton's equations not just remembering them.

The mind could wander or reach a Nirvana type state even an out of body experience was not unknown and experienced by some elite athletes. The out of body experience had been experienced during a night scull coming down a much calmer stretch of water at Chiswick Eyot than Chris Ballieu had masterfully coped with. As the twinkling lights of Hammersmith Bridge's riverside pubs were approaching the Sculler found himself looking down upon himself watching himself scull an experience which was unable to be timed but had gone once navigation around the sweeping bend was needed.

Soon the Black Buoy, Bishops Park and Fulham football Club were growing smaller and The Mile Post had been passed with

Harrods Depository looming, the Scullers body was loosening up and the effortless rhythm was becoming established. On the left there were impressive buildings made of glass overlooking the Thames and soon Hammersmith Bridge with its impressive suspension would arrive then passed the A.R.A (Amateur Rowing Association) and the Sculler would wonder if the chief coach Penny Chuter was watching him scull passed or even the Team Manager whose face the Sculler imagined to be beneath his feet each time he sprang at the catch, pushing the one who had tried to ban him into the dust.

Penny Chuter had been a good sculler in her day and had taken control of a very male dominated sport. She did not carry the equality shown to her with her however. She did have deep seated prejudices as to what an oarsman should be. He should be tall, muscular and in Britain unless demonstrably better, of at least middle class stock. She was a stocky woman and had short mousy brown curly hair and usually a tanned leathery face.

She did have a nice smile but it was rarely seen.

The year before had been a good year bar one mistake and an unfortunate illness at the senior World Championships. The Sculler had been in a coxed four truly a rower's boat before having been moved into an eight which had plotted a rebellion. The eight was comprised of mixed abilities and the draw at Henley Royal Regatta and the fact that semi-finals were raced on the same day as the final meant that it was a risky prospect so three of the scullers in the eight had reasoned a quad would be a far better option, but leaving Justin who had often turned up to training straight from a night club to be sacrificed. The plan was proved right but the rebellion had been quashed as only the Sculler had stepped forward and left a rebellion of one.

The sculler had been left on his own and for a few days left struggling in a sculling boat which at the time seemed foreign and lonely.

The eight split into fours which looked as uncomfortable and awkward as the single felt to him in the lumpy water between Hammersmith and Putney. He had been approached by Billy Mason the coach and begged to return and agreed only to hear the story how it had been him that begged to come back, but by that time it was too late and of little point to descent.

Bill was about six foot three and a charming, funny but also shy man. With his west London accent he had been part of Thames Tradesmen "Beatles" four and part of a four which were trail blazers as the working class had managed to get a foot hold in a very elitist sport. Bill was all arms and legs and nick named "Squidley Didley" by his crew mates, he had missed out on selection for the Olympic eight that got a silver medal at the Toronto Olympics but was considered the Gold medal that they could have had by those crew mates. That disappointment often weighs heavy on coaches who look to fill what they could not fulfil with others. The eight lost in the final being possibly the quickest boat. The semi-final had been narrowly won but in a time thirteen seconds and a quantum more effort than the other semi-final. That had been the risk and was borne out but it did open up other opportunities.

A Quad was formed with two of the quashed rebellion that went on to win the Under Twenty three World Championships in a final worthy of the keystone cops. On the way to the final the van ran out of fuel and with only minutes to spare they had arrived to a go out there and enjoy yourself prep talk from the aristocratic coach Hugh Matherson, part of the Olympic silver medal eight. Then in a strong cross wind they had been started not straight and lost their blades and two lengths to the field and with a charge of the Light brigade they had all called for one push after another to win in a dead heat with the French but having gone at least two lengths faster they had been given the gold medals and Mont Blanc fountain pens. Upon the sculler's return home however his father's only comment was:

"It's alright but you didn't earn any money did you?" with that comment something inside the Sculler had snapped

"Well stuff money then!" he had thought.

The win lead to a place in the senior team but with two of the crew falling ill that was not a successful campaign. The Sculler had looked witheringly at others knocked out who went to night clubs but his austerity broke and he had found himself drunk with a woman in his room, but it was not only he who had found him but the team manager! The manager ordered him to leave the camp but with nowhere to go he had disobeyed and as much as for his insolence as the original misdemeanour a plan had been hatched to ban him from further teams.

An empty Hammersmith Bridge disappeared as St Pauls was passed and The Eyot ran alongside on smooth but incoming water.

Then onto the Crossing point and the Bandstand before Barnes Railway Bridge and The White Hart with the fierce current that ripped through its narrow buttresses and always made the sculler shudder inside at the thought of navigating that bridge badly in a strong current.

The Thames at these points known as The Tideway moves through the movement of the tides and at the moment was filling up against the natural flow and when full on could perceive that the still waters had a meniscus as the currents and eddies subsided for a brief time but the walls of the embankments meant that any motor boats wash would rebound and make sculling difficult, Indeed to miss the motor boats of coaches was the main reason for such an early start. Once their wash was gone came the pleasure cruisers and at a bank holiday weekend came flotillas of Gin Palaces heading for the coast on some escapist pilgrimage which did not turn round at Teddington.

During the days outings the Sculler would race the pleasure cruisers who would respectfully not wash him down as long as he could keep up a speed to keep them at bay. Later morning outings would often be accompanied with the expletives who had got out of bed just to sit in the wash of a coach. Night outings were exciting with an empty river and the lights all twinkling and an extra sensation of speed that the darkness brings.

With Barnes Bridge receding Chiswick Bridge approached and by its side Tideway Scullers where there was a chance of catching a coach's wash as by then a good twenty five minutes had passed since the start of the outing although they may head down towards Putney given the incoming tide.

Today was special and the flat water of a high tide was a rare opportunity to really become one with the boat rather than counteract the flow and eddies of the Tideway's stream. By now training pieces had started rather than just paddling. A favourite was pyramids starting at a low rate of twenty strokes a minute for ten minutes then five minutes at twenty two then four at twenty four up to one minute at thirty strokes a minute, although many first outing the sculler preferred to do at a constant half to three quarter pressure and leave the training pieces to the second outing as they were motivation for a tired body to push itself past breaking point. Unfortunately in the days before Western Sports science The Sculler and Mike Spracklen had not realised the low intensity the Russians did or the chemical enhancement that they had.

Circling the hands like a bike chain in reverse, with the hands coming down over the knees lifting the sculls far off the water so that waves cannot catch or knock them and so the boat. Then the hands would start to rise up towards the catch and the scull rolled square ready to take that one piece of toilet paper and drop into a perfect catch every stroke. Sculling along imagining a series of hoops that were to be caught by the poles with hooks on and levered passed with arms like pieces of string just connecting the power of the legs.

The Sculler knew that you push in a sculling boat not pull. Often with an image of a hero to emulate or an opposition to be beaten the Sculler obsessed over getting fitter. So much weight had dropped off him now that his veins could be seen over his six pack and yet still he needed more knowing that the knives that had been drawn only needed the slightest of excuses to be plunged into him.

After Chiswick the river started to narrow and become more provincial and after Kew Bridge Green Parrots could be heard and seen having colonised Kew Gardens. Kew Gardens sat by the river as the river ran along side of and around two sides of the garden. At the corner the Sculler passed the Pink Lodge and then Richmond lock which proved a physical barrier at low tide but now the river flowed above it and the sculler could take in the delights of the Richmond Reach.

Above Richmond lock and the river suddenly becomes quaint with Richmond's impressive town hall backing onto the river and the old stone bridge the Sculler suddenly felt to be outside London and the glass penthouses and above the bridge and the river tramp there was actually meadow alongside the straight bit of river reminding the Sculler of sculling on the Dee in Chester.

Sculling down to Eel Pie Island there is an imposing view of a large hill in Richmond with impressive buildings sat on it. Eel pie Island where the inventor invented the clock work radio leads to a short trip and then Teddington lock separates the Tideway from the Kingston reach with continues up to Hampton Court. With the tide almost at the top the Sculler has the tantalising prospect of a still full tide and a scull where you can really feel the boat glide on top of flat water, really feel getting hold of the catch and not make any adjustments for flowing lively water. Turning round after over an hour sculling and over an hour to go the Sculler feels tired but satisfied:

"All money in the bank!" as Billy Mason used to say. Bill the coach who'd seen the sculler through a junior year and through last year but the lie had left a bad taste.

The scull back held on top of the bubble was exhilarating with puddles being pushed back and the stern hardly checking at the catch there was an almost perfect synergy of sculler boat and water which made the early start all worthwhile. As Hammersmith Bridge went by there were cars and vans queuing and the sculler thought:

"Why do they do it?" as at the same time in some sort of brave new world hard workers probably thought why does he do it? Back at the club the scull was landed and wearily lifted up to the club. Billy Mason was outside IC.

"Training already done?" He asked in a chirpy way.

"First outing" The Sculler replied.

"Go home, no one can take all this punishment!" Billy said wisely but the Sculler could not hear the advice driven as he was. He would have something to eat and a cup of tea and then be out again in a few hours.

The Training Camp

The Sculler had been put in a pair at trials with a softly spoken partner nick named "Can't be" as his surname was "Heard". Mark was a nice guy but at six foot five and rangy he was not the right partner especially as both of them were naturally bow side. The Sculler swapped sides and did his best and did get through the trial even though he'd won the sculling trial rowing was preferred then and the best three scullers all who had been in the quad that won the gold the year before were put into a young eight and sent to Italy on a two week training camp with a race at Piedaluco regatta to finish off.

Being chosen to row in the British squad eight was bitter sweet for the sculler who had never had a truly positive experience of rowing in an eight. The arrival at the airport was exciting though being greeted by a couple of likely lads, one of whom was the likeable Terry O'Neil. Terry's most obvious and striking feature was his broad cockney smile and accompanied with his confident East London charm. The eight consisted of very young rowers most of whom the Sculler knew and respected as they had been at junior World Championships together and there was soon an enjoyable buzz smiles and chatter of a team on the move.

Two guys had been included in the eight who had not had to go through the cold blustery and questionable trial results at the docks in East London (which is now adjoined by the City airport and in close proximity to Canary wharf.) Both were talented and both had international gold medals at different World Championships but because the boat race had been the week before the trials they had been excused trialling.

Matt and Jim were welcomed and their pedigree could not be questioned both were very sociable and well spoken, having gone to Public schools and now were being refined at Cambridge. Older and more distinguished members of the Great Britain squad also travelled to train in warmer climes and the University of London squad also travelled with the GB team. All were familiar to each other having spent times together as youths during camps and trials. None however had any idea of just how picturesque their destinations would be or what life changing experiences they would have.

The journey through check in, the flight and the coach journey were all a blur as old friends and foes chatted and laughed having made the cut. Some reflected on the privilege and the fact that some equally talented oarsmen had been left at home but the excitement of a two week camp in Italy one could not help but feel that this was living the dream.

When the bus started to arrive at the final destination interest was pricked and through the evening dim light a small sea side style town was seen with a few bars and restaurants and a few local lads who instantly became rivals with their Italian style and looks. The small town was passed through and then the bus crossed a low level bridge across a long six kilometre lake that ran off into the distance and reached the foot of a large volcano.

"Wow!!" and gasps rang out around the bus for the view and the expanse of beautiful water so inviting without current and when calm a permanent meniscus when the oarsmen and scullers could really get hold of the water and transfer power without the wit needed on the tideway. This was more than living the dream!!!!

The bus crossed the bridge with its load of excited adolescents and equally excited elder statesmen and pulled up a short hill to reveal the coast and a four mile long beach that also ran to the volcano only hundreds of yards from the edge of the lake. As the Mediterranean Sea stared back at the a gasp crews the bus turned right and with more gasps and whoops of exhilaration pulled in to a beach front hotel.

"You're joking this is where we are staying?" rang out as oarsmen used to having to share beds in seedy back street hotels in Ghent were treated to the high life.

The reception was not too large and grand but could fit a whole team and the bags which had been eagerly retrieved from the belly of the bus, like a shark slit open on a dock or a deck it had spit out its contents onto the carpark like seagulls following a trawler keen eyed owners had retrieved their bags quickly wanting to see the inside of the white washed hotel. The whole hotel was laid with a creamy white marble and the walls were also white washed with dark wooden doors leading to a large dining hall with red and white checked table cloths.

The stair way lead up to the rooms which also had dark brown doors and twin single beds, reflecting on it now the hotel was probably geared up for training camps and summer holidays. The Russians were already training here but billeted in a different hotel. Most of them including Mikhail Ivanov were members of the Red Army and after this camp would be heading off to the Black Sea for a further three month camp. They lived the life every day!

In the lobby room mates were allocated as members of the team explored the dining room and surveyed the surroundings and the site of this palace, too excited to wait in disciplined order for instruction. The management did not mind and the two cockney lads managed the crowd like two barrow boys, Terry with his suave appearance and broad white smile and Mike with his curly combed back auburn hair and artful dodger swagger.

"Now you two together." The order was given out. No one would insult another by being openly disappointed.

The Sculler was not put with his would be rebellion partner and Juniour World Championship partner Mick Burritt. Mick had olive skin and his skinny, rangy six foot two frame had started to fill out although the sculler could still beat him easily over a seven minute piece Mick had a talent for longer pieces and could return the favour to his stockier comrade.

As a double they were formidable and could easily beat Olympic champions Redgrave and Holmes in a pair during training over seven minutes which is roughly the time taken for an international small boats race, even though Redgrave and Holmes had trained with the Belgium Olympic silver medal double Croix and Deloof and beaten them; the Sculler's lack of favour had seen this partnership devalued.

Mick was more polished in his speech than the Sculler who had moved south to London from the Northern Satanic mills and while the Sculler enjoyed living in London held some of the old countries prejudices and attitudes at the time, which made him talented as a sculler but unruly under upper class authority. Mick was truly middle to upper middle classed and a Catholic which had lead him to be raised by Jesuits. The Sculler had joined him at his school for a few weeks but lasted a short while after the first day welcome

"I didn't want you at this school and you are not welcome!" he was told by the Jesuit head of sixth form. The Jesuit got his wish after only a few weeks saw the Sculler truant and down at the Embankment with Billy Mason helping to paint blades and watching the tides and on some mornings Seb Coe run passed. The sculler loved sculling and was described as poetry in motion by some but his Northern aggression and accent plus his misdemeanour left him there only by his cousins grace.

The proposed ban was lifted only after his cousin said that he would also be included in the ban and as a World senior silver medallist and pair partner to Martin Cross an Olympic Gold medallist the ban was reluctantly lifted but again he was not really welcome, only now he didn't play truant but fought back every stroke pushing the face of the team manager through the bottom of the boat.

The Sculler was paired up with the twenty three year old man of the crew Steve Turner. As most of the crew was Nineteen or Twenty Steve was considered old by the rest of the crew but he was a very likeable and sensible guy. He came from near Henley and had massive feet! He was nick named "Big Foot" very quickly but his pleasant demeanour matched well with the Sculler's more maniac and obsessive character. When the Sculler reached the room Steve with his broad shoulders freckled skin and blonde hair was neatly arranging his kit. The Sculler threw his bag down like an IRA truck bomb it would explode with little warning later when the kit was needed.

The eight which had been chosen had the scullers at each end of the boat. The Sculler had been put at two just in front of the bow man Simon Larkin, the two had been the stroke and three of the successful quad the year before but dispatched to the bows they both had the technical ability to catch hold of the water from a rising bow and like soldiers on a battlefield did what was asked of them efficiently and without complaint. This eight set off huddled in clumps and straggled along with members of other crews soon after the evening meal of pasta and a bread crumbed veal steak which had been consumed with excited chatter.

The first place that was visited was the landing jetties and then the group spread out from the boating area to discover the charms of the bars and restaurants. Italian locals sat faces weather like leather outside drinking coffee and looking bemused as such white tall misshaped people wandered their town in self-discovery. The three man who sat in front of the Scullers stocky six foot one's frame was six foot eight! Colin was a nice guy and also from a working class background. Colin had not made it as a Juniour but had started to flourish once his body got used to its size and he had been coached along with some other talented oarsman. Colin had won gold in the coxed four at the championships in Hamburg the year before.

The rest of the crew ranging around six foot five to the Scullers one were average for rowing circles but not for the fishermen who sat outside the café's but who must have been used to seeing foreign rowers arriving. The crew members all grew tired slowly and in groups they returned across the bridge with its exquisite view down the lake to the hotel and bed. There would be a six am alarm in the morning and training would start. There is no such thing as a free lunch as they say.

The morning arrived and keen oarsman pulled on their kit ready to try out the lake but a strong wind had blown up in the night and meant that the tranquil lake of the night before had become impossible to row upon as the wind headed down from the volcano and large rolling waves with furious white horses crashed against the boating pontoons. Undaunted and determined that the first day should be a success Penny Chuter decided that all these misshapen giants should run down to the volcano and back along the beach.

The run was an eight mile run but bogged down by sand the run became heavy, especially to rowers who now used ergo's (rowing machines) to push up there training volume and were not used to running. Some ran on the firmer sand by the water's edge others kept their feet dry. Those that kept their feet dry some from UL and some from Cambridge suffered injury that plagued them through the first week of the training camp. The injury list made the run look like folly, especially when there was a perfectly good tarmacked road that ran in between the lake and the shore. Folly was often close with the ARA taking the amateur part of their title to heart.

The next day fared better and at last the oarsmen or crippled versions of the oarsmen they had been got into the boat. Colin had a problem getting into the boat as he was so tall and the Sculler found fitting into such a tall crew left him stretching past the points he had ever stretched before, but under Terry's cheerful guidance the crew came together. Over miles and miles the eight passed tributaries or spurs that looked so inviting to investigate but with the cox in command the course was set. The spurs and the ends of the lakes had fishermen's nets who lived an idyllic life of tending these nets in the shadow of the dormant volcano. The water was a pale blue and the murky and unthinkable water of the Thames was pushed stroke by stroke out of memory as the eight started to knit together.

An eight moves much faster than a small boat like a single and rather than a press and squeeze the legs have to be that much faster to get hold of the work and the finish pushed that much harder but little by little the rabble, made up of this team and that got it. There were some examples of fine rowing displayed as the week or so in Sabaudia drew to a close. The combination of three light fast scullers and five big talented oarsman really started to click and gel and Terry was often all smiles at the end of the week.

The last few days of the trip would be spent in Piedaluco to the North of Rome but the camp was held over the Easter period and Martin Cross the athletes representative and devout Catholic insisted that the athletes be given Easter Sunday off and have a trip to Rome. Amazingly he won his argument and even though all did not venture to Rome they would have a rest day for the effects sandy run to finally leave their poor knees. The trip to Rome was on and a victory for the athletes and their wounded knees. The trip started by sitting in the back of the Great Britain squad flat back truck used to pull the trailer of boats and as it rocked down rough roads it was really fun and a true sense of adventure was added.

Zara who went to Oxford, one of the women's squad sat opposite the sculler and she had the most amazing green eyes which then turned out to be contact lenses. Zara was zany and whacky and only added to the sense of adventure as her slightly crazy laugh filled the air in the back of the flat top under a warm Italian Easter sun, until a small provincial railway station was reached. This did not have the high life but it was living the dream as like back packers we were led by Martin to Rome with the faithful.

The train came in soon and Martin who was a teacher became "Sir" with his timetable in hand he navigated from the rolling coastland hills to the middle of Rome. Martin had unkempt hair and was also not much over six foot but had very strong legs after years of training and if Steve at thirty three was old then Martin would have been seen as ancient having an Olympic Bronze, an Olympic gold and a World silver medal which was not gold only by the narrowest of margins. All this meant that he could only be held in high regard. Martin however was very down to earth and he had not sought the day off for himself but for the whole team. He had an easy unpretentious air and a very broad and impish smile but a serious frown when serious. Martin had also been part of Thames Tradesman coming after Billy Mason he was not from an elitist background.

Soon the British team found themselves thronging down to Saint Peter's Square with the faithful and the anticipation of the crowd was contagious. There was faith that could be felt in the air and when in the centre of the square as seeing the Polish Pope addressing the crowd the day off seemed very worthwhile even to a purist like the Sculler. There was time to go into the Vatican but given one could not enter in shorts half the team gave up the chance to see the interior. The sculler was one of them but the faith he talked about was recalled by his Catholic aunt when he himself found faith in Christ.

With the Vatican and Saint Peters Square done the team made it to the Coliseum and the Circus maximus where there were discarded condoms all around. There was also a trip to the river that meanders through Rome and with a full day done tired day trippers made a satisfied way home with a new experience outside the confines of a boat.

The last few days of the camp in Sabaudia had minds wandering to a race but the crew was going well and although they didn't know how quick they were the technique was more than passable and the puddles were being sent more than a good distance passed the stern. There was reason for optimism and Terry was vocally very supportive to the crew.

The boat was de rigged, that is the riggers taken off and the seats taken out and now placed in either the trailer of the flat back which had become a beast of burden rather than freedom. Kit bags were packed and final meals eaten at breakfast, croissants cereals and meats were consumed. The belly of another bus was filled by bags before a trip to the North of Rome. Italy is beautiful. There were rolling agricultural fields before the bus reached the mountain which were spectacular. A Castle perched on a slither of rock as the road wound round unbelievable scenery, by sheer drops and high peaks, tunnels and villages this was more than a training camp this was an experience.

Piedaluco was equally impressive although the hotel was half an hour drive away in a town on a plateau. The Italian team and the famous Abagnale brothers were also staying in the same hotel. The Sculler watched in a sense of awe as the stroke man of the Olympic champion pair packed away three plates of pasta. The Sculler had watched them win the World Championships in coxed pairs in nineteen eighty one in Munich and was now sat with them in the same dining room. At the same championships he had watched Kolbe destroy the field in single sculls and had visualised him for years, the way he moved, the sense of the boats lack of pitch had all been inspirational and the Abagnale's had some of Kolbe's sheen on them to him.

The first outing at Piedaluco was amazing. As the eight went down to the reed bed on a natural two thousand meter lake a large mountain with a pale stone monastery town loomed in the distance dominating the view. Then as the course passed by a medieval town tumbled down over the edge of the course, overhanging a pale stone wall spectators hang off the wall cheering crews on through the races. The outing was joined with extra pressure as Mike Spraklen and Penny Chuter joined Terry in the launch to look at this young eight.

Near the end of the outing Terry really dressed down the eight betraying the trust that he had gained from the young lions. It felt unreasonable to the Sculler and bit of the last year where Billy Mason had lied to the crew mates. It only confirmed how crew rowing and coaches were not to be trusted and the single was again a safer option where there was no one else to deal with.

The race itself was against a full international field with the Italians and over achieving Danish lightweights. Out of the blocks the young lions flew at a great pace driven on impressively by Matt in the stroke seat. The sculler could hardly catch his breath as the Italians and the young British eight started to leave the rest of the field behind. It was a charge that a sculler was not used to. The speed and noise was exciting and as the line loomed the Italian World silver medallists headed the young eight dressed down so badly by a coach they had trusted and worked so hard for by only half a length. It was a great moral victory for the young eight, thrown together destroyed on a sandy beach and betrayed, but then at the medal podium the Italians were disqualified at their own regatta for swapping the stroke man without notifying the authorities. The young Lions got the gold medal accompanied with boos from the Italian crowd but hey got play by the rules.

After the race Mike Spraklen gave an inspiring talk about training four hours a day and the Sculler had listened. Mike Spraklen was there as Redgrave and Holmes were there to race at the regatta also. They had not been on the Sabaudia training camp but had come from a different place. They were half the Olympic gold medal four who were now looking for a second Olympic medal as a pair. They had already won a gold at the World Championships but had two and a half years to wait for the next Olympics.

On the flight back the Sculler found himself sat next to Andy Holmes. Andy was an impressive man with a good six foot four and very broad shoulders with a large chest. He had a reputation of being a hard man being a black belt in martial arts but was cultured and controlled, not brash or aggressive. The Sculler had a reputation of being a fighter having turned up to junior trials with a black eye once. A result of a long standing vendetta as he had inadvertently grassed up a local gang for stealing a man's clothes and wallet at the Northern lake where he had learnt to row and scull. It was also the result of wanting to be out of the family home and his father's constant bullying. Not long after take-off the first words of conversation were exchanged.

"So did it piss you off?" the Sculler asked impishly.

"What?" replied a rather shocked Andy Holmes.

"Redgrave being given a CBE but you got nothing?"

Andy Holmes studied the face of the cheeky Sculler from the North and saw no malice or mockery just actual concern for the injustice done to him.

"No, but I was disappointed that Mike Spraklen got nothing and we were the second gold medallist crew he has coached." (The first being Hart and Ballieu, the sculler and ex Cambridge blue who had mastered a choppy Eyot.) He replied humbly and honestly. After that the conversation flowed easily and the two found a genuine liking for each other.

A Break In Villas.

After a shower, a weight check (It was not uncommon for the Sculler to lose seven pounds in a morning session) and a change of kit the Sculler went to Manuel's the baker on the Lower Richmond Road, passing the pretty painted Georgian terraces that fell down to the river. Manuel's was an inviting shop on the corner of one of the tributary streets to the embankment and Lower Richmond Road. It was double aspect and had an array of temptations that tasted as good as they looked especially after a two and a half hour scull.

The next street along was Festing Road which was renamed Festive Road in a favourite children's program of the nineteen seventies in Britain, Mr Ben. Mr Ben used to leave his house in his bowler hat with a brief case but pop into a costume shop probably based on the Lower Richmond Road. A shop keeper dressed in a Fez would offer different costumes which Mr Ben would try on in the changing rooms, but then be transported to an environment where that costume was from, so for instance a Red Indian costume would land Mr Ben into an adventure with Red Indians and Totem poles.

Mr Ben had all sorts of adventures dressing up and being someone or something else until the shopkeeper appeared. The Sculler had been someone else on the training camp, having croissants for breakfast every morning after the first session meant that croissants were certainly on his menu along from Mr Bens street. Rather like Mr Ben the Sculler went into a house next door to Imperial College's boat hose and had a cup of tea and something to eat in "Villas", and experienced being in another world.

The house Holt Villas was next door to Jack Holt's sailing shop. Jack Holt's family lived on the end house as the Sculler discovered when his daughter made amorous advances towards the Sculler. She was not tall with mousy brown highlighted hair and was cute in a quirky way. She had told him that unfortunately Jack had passed on but in a coincidence Jack Holt's factory was in the next town in a Northern mill next to Littleborough. The Sculler found it ironic that he had travelled from the mills of the North but found himself a neighbour to a mill owner.

Villas had first been experienced by him when the students kept goldfish in the bath and for the first six weeks of living there they had used newspaper instead of toilet paper before a rota and pooled money system had domesticated eight young lads.
Domesticated to a fashion: they had still thrown a TV out of the lounge window to see if the vacuum would implode, they had seen how long they could go without cleaning the grill pan, even putting out the fire by blowing on it while grilling pork chops. Eventually there was a system which taught all to cook and wash up. Every fourth day two would have to wash up and cook for the other

eight. It did lead to an ability to cook for the Sculler.

Villas had been a world he had spent a year in as a stranger having lived in the house with Imperial College student rowers but not being at University he had felt out of place. A message had been left in his folder

"Fuck off to Smallsville" a reference to his Northern town left as it turned out by Mick Burritt. At the time however it hurt as the Sculler had not known who write it or if it was a corporate statement.

Later finding out it was his old partner Mick meant the blow was easier as Mick had resented him coming down to where he had been nick named "Super Juniour" only to be over shadowed by a younger Juniour and the Sculler had been unsympathetic when he cried after they had lost out on a bronze medal even agonisingly close to the gold after Mick had contracted Bronchitis.

The Sculler had already leant to win and lose with dignity, more so than his privileged peers who's sense of entitlement made loss unpalatable. The drive to win was made of steel inside the Sculler, not that winning meant all but a fear of losing drove him on, not to hear his father's mocking dug deep inside him.

"Did you lose?" had greeted him when he had turned over a two length deficit in a dock in Liverpool. It was when the other scullers family had cheered for him. Like a raging bull he had anger locked within him from beatings the privileged did not know about and it raged; he sculled down two lengths in two hundred meters. His black eye which horrified the rowing world was met with glee by his father at the thought someone had hit his "parasite" son. As a child he had been sat on a sofa with his father and younger brother taunting all laugh at the Sculler. Being on your own was easy and there was little comfort being part of the teams on offer. The single would do just fine, even if those that hated him rocked in his wake when the dare line up against him rather than with him.

Mick Burritt had been left ten seconds behind which was a different league of class according to Billy Mason. An Oxford blue and Simon Larkin had seen his speed over the regatta course at Nottingham, in fact he had not been beaten in any regatta race in the single but in crews, as part of teams he had tasted defeat and knew that it was not good but a lesson to be learnt, a motivation for future training sessions. There is no shame in being beaten but one should never lose, one should never give up, never give someone the victory but make them earn it.

Villas was still a place that tolerated him however. He had been there when Billy Mason bought pies and cakes from Manuel's in celebration for being alive. Bill had got into his launch with the crews up by the mile post but when the engine started the launch had jumped and in freezing conditions and bogged down by heavy clothing Squidley had used his long arms to grab hold of one of the chains of the string of boats facing the Black Buoy.

"Help, help!!!!" had been heard from Villas by Mick Burritt who for some reason had not trained that day. Mick commendably sprang into action and saved Bill to everyone's relief. Bill for weeks sat in Villas telling the young how they don't appreciate life and that one doesn't until it is nearly snatched away.

That day the Sculler sat between outings eating his delicious Manuel's steak pie. The North may be famous for pies but you would have to go a long way to beat Manuel's steak pie. He was eating his fruit loaf and eating croissants in Villas lounge. Billy was not in the lounge at the time but busy in the boat house. In the lounge was Little Nige and Tom a non-rowing member of the house.

They were chatting and the Sculler was talking about how the sculling was going and how he didn't have a gauge of how fast he was going.

"I've never done the single Internationally, I'd love to know how fast I Am." he commented.

Within a minute of saying that the phone rang and Tom told the Sculler that the call was from him and it was Penny Chuter the National coach.

"Hello its Penny here."

"Yes"

"I'd like you to do the single at Mannheim Regatta, not the eight." She said cautiously hoping the sculler would not be too disappointed.

"That's amazing!!!! I've just said that I'd like to do the single internationally!!!" gushed the Sculler to a bemused and pleased National Coach.

Having put the phone down the Sculler was ecstatic.

"I'm doing the single!!! That's amazing!!!" The Sculler called to the Holt Villains as they liked to call themselves. There was genuine excitement in Villas as the Sculler was up for it and as training mates they knew that he was capable of anything.

For most people being put on the spot, on your own with a full international field would lead to absolute fear. Many talented crew oarsmen could not cut it in the caldron of pressure in the single, where there were no touching of hands. No one to turn to when that dread and fear gripped before a race. When that

"Why am I here?" moment grips before the start, when one fears the pain you are about to put yourself through. The Sculler however was comfortable with it. No one to blame, no one to mess it up and no one else to take the credit or be given the credit, just you, the boat and the water.

The tiredness disappeared and soon the Sculler was back on the water and a trip to

Kew ensued with power sculling in pyramids. The focus of being put to the test gave extra pressure onto the stretcher and the team manager's face. Ten minutes at twenty, Five minutes at twenty two ensued and by the time he was back at Putney he had done his four hours but stayed still despite Billy's protests. The Sculler did not go home but waited to do a third outing but on a lumpy high evening tide awash with launches and other crews and scullers. The Sculler however did not make it past Hammersmith, or the ARA, but crest fallen knew that he had done enough and limped home so tired that he could hardly master the swell.

Terry O'Neill washed him down with a broad smile and a wave as he saw the new eight out on the water. The three light fast scullers had been taken out and three lumps replaced them. They were big but were those who sat in a boat not on top of it. All from Oxford they had avoided the trials and one "Row like Me" sat with a chiselled jaw like a well-spoken Buzz Light Year in the middle of the eight. Suddenly the call made sense and Penny had gone back to type, but none of that mattered to the Sculler who had got an unexpected and welcomed chance to prove himself.

The next day brought another opportunity as the sculler met Tony Reynolds, Little Nige's elder brother. Tony was one of the only people who won the Lucerne regatta but did not get the chance to represent his country that year. Tony a bright physics teacher had been the bow man of the Cambridge Blue Boat that infamously hit a Black Buoy before the start of the Boat Race meaning that the race had to be postponed embarrassingly till the Sunday. Again and again the shot is shown on television with Tony's curly blonde hair and a worried look as the bow of the boat was raised at forty five degrees from the horizontal. It was not Tony's fault but his face is in shot.

Tony was a good and accomplished oarsman who could scull and the two of them agreed to do an outing together that week so that the Sculler could get a gauge of his current speed. The piece was from Chiswick Bridge to Barnes Bridge which would take about three and a half minutes and be half an International race. The piece started and the Sculler left Tony for dead and at the end of the piece the distance between them was too large to estimate. The Sculler was going well.

Having to race in Manheim meant that his boat would have to go a few days before the race to be trailered by the flat back that had taken them to the station to Rome and Saint Peter's square. This was a blessing in disguise as the Sculler was forced to rest as the intensity of his training was too high for the time he was doing it. Chris Ballieu was a lawyer, Martin Cross a teacher, his cousin worked in construction and so the British training regimes were intense, as they had to be fitted around jobs. The sports science revolution had not happened and so four hours at the intensity only known to the Brits was too hard, just as Billy Mason had warned. Billy was a visionary within rowing and read running magazines and gained knowledge from more developed sports.

Mick Burritt had been picked to row in a coxless four, with Richard Stanhope, one of the Scullers boyhood heroes, which was prestigious selection but he kindly said that the Sculler could use his boat. Mick's boat was a Janousek which felt foreign and so the Sculler enjoyed a few days of rest.

Those days building up to the departure were days filled with excitement, anticipation and visualization of the upcoming performance? The Sculler's poor girlfriend was strangled several times as when sleeping in his arms he did racing starts in his sleep strangling her at the "finish" inadvertently!

The days passed soon enough and again a Heathrow departures lobby was filled with chatter. The Sculler had no crew or coach but was happy enough as he knew all the team and was in the boat that he wanted to be. He recounted the coincidence many times, as it had been just what he had said that he wanted, All the Embankment knew and friends from Thames Rowing club tracked his progress in the broad sheets keen to see how he would do.

The team was literally billeted in an Army Barracks which were an imposing grey with a large iron gate, there were no twin rooms and had bunk beds six to a room. Soon they were down to the course. This was not Piedaluco this was industrial and the large barges on the river Rhine were looming with iron and steel but not like the monastery town at Piedaluco. The course was on a dock with large iron cleats along the side. Docks can be tricky as the swells from the umpires launches can rebound and leave a rolling surface to scull on, like trying to run a fifteen hundred meters on a water bed if you like.

The warm up scull went well with the sculler paddling a few lengths of the docks at quite a faster pace than others around him as he was fresh and ready to go.

Lightweight?

Not having a coach or crew left some logistical issues, for instance having to book in to registration as there was no coach to do it for you and where to be put. The Sculler was put with Nottingham County Rowing association which was fine as they were Northern and he had lived in Nottingham while training in Nottingham the year before in the quad scull. They had a more irreverent attitude and the spirit was much more club boys on tour with jokes and messing about.

The morning duty was to sign in and after standing in line the Sculler reached the front where a heavy set six foot five middle aged man with a middle age spread took his details.

"Great Britain under Twenty three single." The Sculler dutifully reported.

"Lightweight?" asked the large German.

"No heavyweight." The Sculler replied. The large German started laughing at him. This riled the Sculler, suddenly the street fighter awoke. All laugh at….rang in his ears, the beatings and the mockery of his childhood ignited. "Lightweight? I'll fucking show you lightweight!!!!" He thought but did not give the German the satisfaction of a reaction, but seethed inside, as he took his number from the mocking German.

The heat found the Sculler lined up against Man Mountain a Romanian sculler who had a body like Arnold Schwarzenegger. The sculler recognised him from the junior World Championships in Sweden when Mick Burritt and he had nicknamed him, but his unlikely under eighteen frame was made young by the Russian coxless fours greying hair! It was the year of the Soviet Olympic boycott and the seniours needed to go somewhere. Every sculler could be amazing in the Scullers eyes as no coaching or investigation of the field had gone on. All he knew is that the first two got to the final.

The start left the Sculler and Man Mountain a Juniour World champion in coxed pairs leading the field and at half way they were neck and neck, with the rest of the field falling well behind. Man Mountain then put in a push on the still dock and pulled a boat length out of the sculler. The Sculler surveyed the field and was comfortably in front and decided to keep his powder dry, as second was good enough. The two scullers maintained the same cruise speed until five hundred meters to go when Man Mountain pulled out another length with another push giving his predictable game plan away. Again the Sculler let him go. The Sculler had enough to reach the final and there were no medals on offer in the heat. At the finish line the Romanian beat the Sculler by two lengths but the sculler knew that he had another ten seconds locked away. If the Romanian had more than six then he was too quick but did he have another six?

The Sculler got the bus back to the barracks and after eating lay on his bunk staring at the bunk above visualizing the race. The Nottingham boy's high spirits had become annoying but he cut them out and stared intensely ahead. The rhythm, the race rhythm flowed through him. The start, three quarter stroke squeezed then two fast half strokes quick with the legs then lengthen out over ten strokes to full length then keeping the pace up start to settle into the rhythm floating on top of the boat feeling the boat fly underneath you, lifted out of the water truly gliding on the meniscus. His shoulders could rock in the rhythm his biceps could feel the finish, his whole being could spring at the catch. Fucking lightweight!!

The Sculler did not visualise winning, just his race, just getting from A to B as quickly as he could. That is all you can do. During the race you can read the race. You can dig deeper but all you can do is prepare to give all. Prepare to get from A to B like your life depended on it. Anyone who had more, give them respect but never lose, never give less than you've got, never lose. All you can do is put yourself in the place where pain is ignored or even welcomed and eaten as fuel. The burn not endured but pushed through and enjoyed. The speed of the boat, the rhythm, the rhythm, the rhythm, all about the rhythm.

The fact that there was a head wind was put out of his mind as heavier scullers have an advantage into head winds or so accepted rowing knowledge would believe. He set himself one target just beat man mountain. The Romanian was perfect for Penny Chuter another Row like me but one with the guts to show himself in the single at least. He would pay with his obvious heavyweight credentials. The Sculler would show him what a "lightweight" could do. The Sculler was riled and ready to kill out there on a German dock.

When the Sculler got down to the dock there was a very strong headwind blowing straight down the dock. It was so windy that he struggled to control the boat on his head while carrying his sculls in his right hand. Mick Burritt saw him struggling and left his four and took the blades from him and let him control the boat with two hands on the riggers. As they went down to the pontoon at the half way point of the course Andy Holmes looked up from checking the boat and simply said:

Have a good one!" with a smile. The Sculler with tunnel vision like Mike Tyson entering the ring simply nodded. Down at the pontoon Mick Burritt had one thing to say:

"Just beat Man Mountain!"

"That's all I'm planning to do!" The Sculler replied to his should be doubles partner, slightly surprised that they both saw that as a target worthwhile independently of any consultation. They had not even said a word to each other and yet they both were on the same page. Without the knives that were drawn, indeed the knives that probably saw him in the single, it would be the obvious boat for both of them, but at this time the single was the place to be.

The Sculler sculled down to the start where the other scullers and he circled each other like sharks waiting for a kill. Eyeing each other up to check for potential or weakness like they were punters eyeing up on who to bet on. The Sculler was wearing his Italian International top, with its echoes of Italia, Italia, Italia, booming out. For some reason there was a delay and as the delay was prolonged and during it the eye of the storm passed over and the dock fell calm.

"Game on!" the Sculler thought to himself as the heavyweights advantage had disappeared. The delay however was prolonged further enough for the wind to pick up to be a strong tail wind which would give him the advantage and effectively shorten the course meaning that a fast first thousand was good, as the water may limit the work able to be put on in lumpy water. The sculler looked up and said:

"Thank you" to a God he as yet did not believe in and he kissed his Italian badge.

With the distant arrival of an umpires launch speeding towards them, down the dock wall next to the Scullers lane, the starter called the scullers forward. Without a coach the Sculler did not know the ins and outs but he did know that there were at least four World Champions lined up including him. As the launch arrived the starter set them off.

The first few strokes of the start were met with the wash from the umpires launch and the Sculler got his blades caught badly in the water (A crab). He glanced round to see the other scullers leaving him behind.

"You've come this far just have a good scull." Immediately popped through his mind and he relaxed and started to scull loosely and fluently in a rhythm that left strain behind. Often during the fastest sculls or rows you do feel like you are not really trying as the rhythm is so in tune with the boat there is hardly and weight to pick up and it is though you are tapping a bike wheel along in the dark with a knitting needle, just tap and go, tap and go.

At five hundred meter the sculler looked out of his boat and his rhythm briefly to see that he had taken back the deficit and now had a two length lead over the field! Man Mountain in the next lane was labouring with his musclebound frame in his wake and the others were fairing not much better. At half way where the pontoons and boating area was he was five lengths and ten seconds clear as the water became lumpy he saw Man Mountains riggers catching the peaks of the waves as Man Mountain sat in the boat and let his boat sit in the water. The Sculler like Chris Ballieu let his boat sit on the peaks of the waves and tapped along in synergy with boat and synchrony with the waves.

This was the point that Man Mountain had pushed and now not needing to keep any powder dry the Sculler pushed on but in doing so tightened up to give the extra effort. Immediately his left scull crabbed and swang his boat a good twenty degrees out of line of the straight lane giving the others who were already tight a chance to catch up. Tapping his boat straight as a loud cheer and laugh rang out from the boating area he continued for ten strokes back in the rhythm and started once more to pull away and then tried another push to get back what he had lost but his scull started to crab again. He relaxed and stopped the crab:

"Just keep doing what you've been doing" he thought.

The Sculler was still believing that the World Champions would come back, that they had not expended the energy that he had. He had forgotten that he was also a World Champion and saw those in the field as better. With paranoia he pushed on loosely until seven hundred and fifty meters to go when an over powering feeling, belief and even arrogance gripped him

"No, I'm fucking going to win this one!" He thought and still loosely and fluently he began to stamp down on the stretcher and leave them behind struggling as they were with the lumpy water and white horses.

By the time the Sculler reached the last thirty strokes he had over an easily verdict distance and suddenly the effort he had put in gripped him and he simply wound down with an unassailable lead he went down in rate and effort and sculled in for his victory. The next day his friends at Thames Rowing Club would read of his victory.

"The crazy bastard did it!" they whooped and laughed, holding his maverick and intense way with admiration and affection.

The Germanic crowd were not as impressed, peering in astonishment as this six foot lightweight had beaten their six foot eight singles Under Twenty Three World Champion easily and without needing to push for the line. The whole crowd leaned forward in disbelief as his frame lean through countless miles was given the gold and a plaque of Germanic beauty.

The scull back to the pontoons was sweet. He still had not been beaten in the single. Richard Stanhope sat on one of the cleats by some large cranes and just smiled and nodded at the Sculler in approval and admiration. The Sculler had beaten him when he was only seventeen in Chester with Stanhope and the Scullers cousin just back from the Olympics where Martin Cross and Steve Redgrave had won the first Gold of Sir Steve's long and illustrious career.

One of the coaches and Martin Cross' original coach David Tanner stood on the dock side heaping praise but the Sculler did not take it as he knew that his knife was drawn against him along with the team management and it was to be at his winter gym that he was to be excluded originally. It was at those gym sessions that he had been so impressed by the strength of Martin Cross' legs and his determination.

At the pontoon Mick Burritt helped the sculler with his blades and winner's booty. Andy Holmes and Steve Redgrave were still checking the boat. Andy glanced up to see the Sculler's return.

"How did you do?" he shrugged with his right hand open as if it was to grab the result. The Sculler with a large emphatic smile let go of one of the riggers and put up his index finger triumphantly into the air! Andy's eyes widened and a big smile and a nod of "I knew he was a good un" spread over his face as he returned to checking the boat so intricately.

With the boat racked the Sculler was approached by a German reporter:

"What is your name? Asked the reporter. The Sculler duly obliged only to hear.

"You must be used to sculling on the rough water yah?" in a mealy mouthed Germanic search for why the master race had lost. Not you are an excellent technician or a compliment, just reason to affirm that "Row Like Me's should be the master race and "Lightweights" who could scull should not dare to beat them.

The Sculler bought himself a beer and sat on the docks cobbles drinking it watching Redgrave and Holmes still checking their boat.

"Why do they do it?" came into his mind. The Sculler was satisfied, complete and felt vindicated. The childhood ambition that had been seeded into him as an eight year old was fulfilled; to become a World Champion but now in a full international field he had proved against his peers that he was one of the best. It was enough. No longer would

"You only win because you train harder!" from his father seem so frustrating. The knives that sought to destroy him were now blunt and too late. Even then they planned to get him out of the single and put him in a lame quad with a bucket in tow but he had

had his day in the sun even under a rolling grey cloud in Manheim.

The Eight into which the scullers had been removed and the Oxford boys had been slotted came passed way behind the field. Having lost the Boat Race the Oxford boys were teaching the others to "Row Like Me" and accordingly sit in the boat and heave it along. The dance had gone and with it the speed. Good manners don't win races, the fitter the boat stopper the longer he can stop the boat and the fool thinks he knows all but knows not even that all men are ignorant and is ignorant that he is ignorant.

As he drank the beer the pubs that he had run passed started calling with their smell of beer, cigarettes and laughter with their twinkling lights at Hammersmith that outshone the ARA; they said there is more to life than this. What was he missing? The vans that queued over Hammersmith Bridge what did they know that he didn't?

Maybe his father's mockery of the sport he excelled in was working but the elitist world that had rejected him and his Northern traits suddenly saw a jewel but a Jewel that's head was turned. A jewel that life was going to take on another path. A jewel that saw through their silly game but still loved the oneness with the boat and all he had learnt. It was if the shop keeper had arrived to tell Mr Ben it was time to leave this adventure and get on with life's next adventure.

Printed in Great Britain
by Amazon